Secrets & Stars

A poetry collection
by Alix Klingenberg

To love me, you must also love the dark.

To all the people who have loved me whole.

List of Illustrations

Introduction

I went to see the shaman
and she saw the fox first.
The fox who keeps my secrets,
red tail curled around sharp teeth.
She saw my belly,
filled with black balls
of trauma and grief
and quietly removed them
like a string of rotten pearls.

The fox told her
she was not allowed
to know everything,
that many of the tales were
for my ears alone.
And I have since made my way
to that place many times.
The place where I am eternal
and known so deeply.
The place where plants and animals
come close and share
their wisdom with me.

I can travel anywhere while holding
hot tea in my papasan chair,
the drum beat guiding me
to where my soul is needed.

It has made me less afraid of death,
and that is really saying something.

The fox still sits by my side,
a guardian for everything
I cannot say aloud.
She reminds me that secrets
are part of the deal
with being human -
that not everything
can be known or shared.
It is part of the price of embodiment.

Soon, soon I will release again
into the All of things -
release time and form,
but for now,
fox rests her head on my foot
and keeps me quiet company
while I share what pieces I can
in this messy thing we call
poetry.

How Not to Write

There are a million ways to **not** write.

Do the dishes.

Reorganize the spice rack.

Have a baby (this one will get you out of it for years!).

Drink yourself numb every evening (another long-term strategy).

Get really into your job.

Develop 15 other hobbies.

Worry about never being good enough.

Give away your words to other people.

Become obsessed with what or who you might lose (this one is my personal favorite).

Forget where you put that one poem.

Start to write a book and then stop so "you don't ruin it".

Talk to people on the phone.

Social media.

Self-forget.

Try to be perfect.

Try to be successful.

Try to know everything.

Try to be everything to everyone.

There are a million ways to not write.

There is only one way to write: open the page and begin.

Childhood Minnows

I step into the river of time
and feel the years swim past my ankles:
childhood minnows and eels of adulthood.
I lay down on my back and let the eons
take me all the way to the beginning,
to you.

How Poets Are Born

I imagine we all spend an awful amount of time
underestimating ourselves.

Or maybe not all of us,
just those of us who were told,
over and over again
that we could be whatever
we wanted to be.

Only, we can't, can we?

Because what I want is to float around, incorporeal,
and never have to think about eating food
or brushing my teeth.

What I want is to be the living embodiment
of love and mercy,
but instead I scream and throw things if you
cut me off in traffic.

What I want is to name every good thing
the world has to offer
and string together meaningful words that alter humanity
at a cellular level.

But what I'm coming to is that I can't do
any of the things that I want.

Which is maybe how most poets are born.

Light Chaser

The magic carpet went up past the treeline
and I looked over to see where you were.
But you were on another carpet
chasing little balls of light
that floated over the water.

For a moment I wanted to chase you,
to get you over to my carpet.
"Be with me!" my little heart screamed.

But the carpet took me higher
and I flew out past the stars and the sun
and through a veil to a place
where I don't think about you as much.

And I worry that I'll lose you one of these days,
with you always chasing light
and me never veering from the depths.

Unbridled

I can flow and run
alongside the world
making few waves and
smiling my giant smile.
I know how to do that.
To shut things off,
to turn things on,
to read the room,
to stay safe
by being exactly
what you want.

After awhile, though
the stream carves a path
so deep and so fast
that my true nature
rushes along the seaside towns
and gathers enough energy
to destroy unsuspecting villages.

Umbrellas overturned,
whales beached,
and the screams of all those I've fooled...
running from the waves of
my unbridled authenticity.

Gumdrops

I am prone to wandering,
eyes scanning the horizon
for little gumdrops of love.
I find them in clumps
of grass and mountain ledges.

Gathering pockets of sugar,
sweet moments shared.
Little balls of reassurance that this life
is worth the pain and daily stings.

I find my pockets filled of late
and suddenly I can share
instead of stingily clinging
to one or two sticky messes
covered in lint,
savoring each tiny instant,
captured in ink or shadow.

The Take-Over

It took over everything,
creeping up brick walls and
into the earth center
of my being.

It took over with tendrils curling
and wet stems twisting
around my wrists like bracelets.

It clung to my body,
creating definition
around my arms and legs,
while stretching around my throat
and making my words longer.

The power felt green and wet.
It created tunnels inside
the sharp creases of my mind,
all the way to you.

Wrapped around the pieces of you
that you wanted to hide away.
Secrets revealed in the dark,
damp ground,
uncovered bits of humanity,
like bones sucked dry by the worms.

The Call

I am rooted.
A potted plant soaking
in the light from stars.
Kitten whiskers and
bowls of red cherries
on the table.
The feeling of cold tile
on bare feet.

The woods call to me,
filled with the glowing eyes
of wolves and foxes.
They wait for me patiently,
wondering exactly when
I will run with them,
hair down and feet black
with the soil of freedom -
the call of wild winds.

Pushing back my apron
and throwing it on the floor:
the pie can wait,
and the laundry will dry on its own,
and I, I must run
to the dark trees,
to the pack that waits
silently at the edge
of everything
I think is real life.

The Paradox of Travel

I am in-between worlds,
my body here,
my heart split,
and my mind
a million miles away
in lush landscapes
and deeply flowing connection.

It's quite a juxtaposition.

The paradox of travel
is that while it changes everything.
I always find that
I return home
more myself than ever.

Entirely Free

My head is full of flowers
I don't know the names of
and trees with mossy twists of vines.
Roots lift up out of the earth
and create magic doorways for tiny lives.

Banquets of honey and beds of ferns
and dark hair blowing on sweet winds.
Fair hands stained with blackberry juice
and wounds healed with strange melodies
that take the sting away.

My breath comes quickly here.
This beauty makes my heart ache,
stretching muscles that had once
atrophied with civilization and urgency.

And I am slowly pulled apart,
wild green shoots opening
pathways to truer words
and worlds where I
am entirely free.

Like Stars

It was like I knew you in another life.
Desire mixed with nostalgia.
A longing for the past that is also the future.
I was so sure of it somehow,
somewhere in the depths of my mind,
that we had a past,
like stars.

Truth in Motion

There is something about
the curve of your neck
that makes me want
to bury myself in it.
Smell your scent,
the whole essence of you,
so smooth. So perfect.

There is something about
the way your smile goes sideways
that makes me melt
into a puddle of desire.

There is something about
your casual intensity,
and your reflections of grace
I've only seen in my mind's eye,
suddenly present before me.

And I can barely breathe.
I barely see
or stand or function
or even eat,
because I am no longer human
but something more,
and something that needs far less (but more specific)
than I've ever needed anything before.

Like a single, solitary glance from you.
Just a word or, my god, a touch
and I might become every bit
as magnificent as you are.

I am not altogether capable of living without it now:
the whole of you and me.
Bliss and chaos and isometric alignment.
I hear your words come through me
and I know now what love can feel like.
Like truth in motion.

I Fall Asleep

I fall asleep to the sound of rain and cat purrs.
The thrumming of my heart strings
and your voice,
vibrating the tuning fork
of my solar plexus.
I taste you in my dreams,
in red wine and stardust.
I wrap your tongue with mine
and kiss away the fear
that I can never be enough.

Holy Water

I am holy water, the thirst of a thousand setting suns,
and you are a rider on horseback,
squinting into the fading light.

Bound tightly by norms and ideas
of what is sacred and right,
I work to move the needle
of your moral understanding
but I am so soft that I
begin to fall away
at your hard edges.

Coiling around to the back
where the points hurt less
and your smooth skin can't help
but feel the cool love of safety.

Illuminated refractions of myself seen through
layers of imperceptible inaccuracies that add up
to a picture that looks a lot like my twin.

I am a shadow of you,
and I stand behind,
letting the sun remove all traces
of my mystery and grace.

Power of Loss

My right foot is poised
over the edge of the dark waters,
the white spears vanishing
under the surface.
Dangling, falling, down and down,
hair flowing in my face like seaweed
Starfish cling to my back and neck -
I am taken under,
to the fathmic feelings
and the sandy mud of deeper waters -
grief and rage, intense vulnerability.
A charge, electric ...like an eel
or lighting shocking the water.
And I am lit up, completely splayed open
surrendering to the power of loss.

Enough

I've never felt innocent before.
I've never felt new and sweet and plain.
Radiating dimensions of pure light
and iridescent slivers of my original self,
the shiniest peace I've ever felt.
Like worthiness coming up from the earth
and shaking my soul til I stopped screaming for more.
Until I stop wondering, finally, if I am enough.

Kool-Aid

I want to etch you into my skin,
swallow you whole and be swallowed.
I want to run against you and crash inside
like the magic platform in Harry Potter
or the Kool- aid man.
This physical distance is killing me.
My skin aches for your touch,
my heart your heart.
I want just silence and breath
and slowly rising fire.
A heat that becomes unquenchable,
we are fire and fire,
and I am ready to burn with you.

In My Bones

I feel you in my bones,
in my blood
as if my home
is at the center of your being.

A space for me,
my-sized exactly.
I fit in there
and instead of being small
I am larger than I've ever been -
free and infinite and expanding.

Your love has set something off.
I felt it like a tremor in the earth,
fault lines
and oceans of past lives
come crumbling down
and release an energy,
a knowing river,
a current of trust
and ancient promises.

There was no way not to love you,
because I have never
been more present
to the love within myself
as I am when I'm with you.

Out of Stars

I painted your face out of stars,
dipping fingertips
into black and gold dust.
You touched my heart
with flowing hands
of honeyed light,
weaving a sense of belonging
into the fibers.

I want to feel your palms
on my face
like sunlight,
like cool water,
like essential rain
watering tiny unseen roots
that grow along the heart walls.

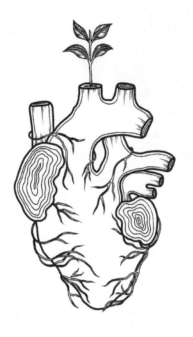

Break-up Mix

I made the breakup mix
at the same time as the one
where I told you
just how much I loved you.
Because I only know
how to feel love this deeply
when I also anticipate loss.

(Thanks dad)

Without Fear

I tiptoe to the door of your heart
and sneak in through the keyhole,
climbing under the soft, white blankets
and kissing your fingertips one by one.
I try not to wake your brain with its
chilly calculations and cutting safety valves.
I smell your skin and wait.
I wait for you to hold me
without fear.

Permission to Exhale

It was my oxygen;
your approval, your gaze, your adoration.
I needed it to breathe.
I plugged myself into your system,
and waited for permission to exhale.

Betelgeuse

They say Betelgeuse
might be exploding soon,
the second brightest star in Orion.

Orion, which is forever
going to make me think of you now.
Exploding soon means it already did of course,
some 600 years ago.

And something about it all feels fitting.
My heart in pieces
and all I can see is the exploded remnants
of what we once were.

Moth Body

I couldn't look away.
I was drawn to him
like a magnet,
my little moth body
throwing itself at the sun.

Little Satellite

My heart
          my heart
                    my heart.
Percussive beats like sonar,
radiating out into the night.
And for a moment I felt yours respond in kind.
An explosion of communication and sharing
of long lost songs and technology.
My little satellite finally reached the edges of space
and there you were.
A signal stronger than I knew existed.

But I can feel you spin away,
being called back to another planet
or simply a denser place in the atmosphere.
And now there's nothing but
the reverberation of my own shaky breath
and the deep black silence of the night sky.
I float away, knowing it will be years again
before my radio catches static,
and lifetimes before I feel heard so clearly again.

So Sure

I was so sure of who I was
before I met you
but now I can see
that the constellation of selves
I'd clustered together
were but a tiny part
of the sky
that is my wholeness.

The End of the Fantasy

I shrink down
to the size of your idea of goodness,
legs everywhere,
my body will not fit in the box.

No matter how hard I try
there are pieces of me
that flail about and disgust you
with their lack of propriety.

I am a mess of limbs and ache
of desire and lust-
a massive pile of flesh and bone.
I am quite quick to pull
in these unseemly bits
for as long as I can hold them.

But you've found me out now.
And the box has been removed.
I am naked and brazen
with wild hair and animal eyes
that arouse you.
The audacity!

I only wanted to be a being who lit you up,
but I can't hide my shadows.
They are what make me real.
And you only want the fantasy
I cannot pretend to be anymore.

Black Cave

There is a little black cave
where my heart once beat.
She packed her bags
and threw the sheets out the window,
absconding in the early hours
before the birdsong.

How easily I loved the world.
How easily I loved you, too -
effortless, cavalier and senseless…
I am haunted and gaunt,
with sunken cheeks and duller eyes.

I guess I got what was coming to me.
For why should anyone get to have
all the candy?
No, I took one handful too many
and now I have seen the way I will fall.
Not in an explosion of anger and grief,
but rather a slow diminishing
of my capacity to love.

Rough

I like it rough.
I like a challenge.
Make me earn your love.
Intermittent reinforcement
and confusing conversations
in which I feel misunderstood.
I recreate it again and again
to try and understand
how to build love out of nothing.

The Poet

The poet inside me wears black and likes
blurry, fine art photography.
She stays up late watching people stumble home
drunk from all the bars.
She leans out the fire escape,
her breath rising like smoke through the cold night air.

The poet inside me wants you to love her
with your hands like butterflies on her face.
She wants you to ask her to sit
in the arm chair
so you can remember her
in that light forever.
She wants you to write films about her,
remembering exact moments
like snapshots when certain songs
come on the radio.

She wants you to know how she likes her coffee,
and hear that you've never felt seen before
the way she sees you.
That Orion had never quite had the same meaning
before,
and that never seeing her eyes again would be sure death.

The poet inside me has tried to write about
anything else all day,
but she is a broken record skipping and
replaying every word you've said
over and over, on repeat.

Catastrophe

This imagination of mine is not meant for catastrophe.
It's meant for slow mornings and bright eyes
that twinkle with the light of exploding stars.

So I'm just going to keep writing love poems
because love is what I know how to do.

Turtle

I wish I didn't need people so much.
That I could be a turtle,
hiding away inside a shell,
cool and dark and safe.

But I live this life on the highest kind of octane.
Skin open to every punch,
bruises covering my legs and arms,
without a shell in sight.

No, I don't need you to reject me with words,
the way you couldn't meet my eyes
has said everything.

And I am torn to invisible shreds,
my outward layers untouched
while my insides bleed
from a thousand tiny ways
I couldn't live up to your standards.

Origami Heart

I folded up my heart into a tiny origami box
and left it on your doorstep to unwrap.
But somehow you missed it there,
all packaged and neat, and now I wonder
what else I've lost along the way
by making it too small.

Lavender and Pine

Your soul calls to me.
I can hear it howling my name
in the night winds
when the moon is hidden
behind rough clouds.

I can hear it whispering to me
in quiet moments
when the texts have stopped
and my heart
wonders if it will ever beat again.

Wild souls floating in the ether,
untethered and joyful,
nuzzling each other's necks and
curling thick tails around each other
until we are one fuzzy ball.

Your soul calls to me even when you muzzle it,
ask it to behave or
demand that it sit
with prim paws in the corner
and obey your stark commands.

It calls to me the loudest then,
when you've forgotten who you are,
a creature of lavender and pine,
of brilliant hues and shades of grey fur.

I call you back home,
heart in my throat,
and hope that one day
the leash will break.

Coming Back to Earth

I tried so hard to understand all of your symbols.
The words you use rather than connecting with reality.
I was taken on an unexpected ride, through the skies -
as you pointed at stars and planets,
and at columns of light and ancient writings in the sand.

And I watched you, so entranced,
then tried on your language,
using your voice to find my own.

I waited patiently for the tour to be over.
Waited for you to turn around and see me.
Waited for you to have the same curiosity
about my stories, but you never did.

And so I disembarked the spacecraft
and took up the shovel and seeds.
Then continued planting my garden,
tending to life here on Earth
and smiling up at the sky,
hoping you would find someone
who shined as brightly
in your mind's eye
as you did in mine.

The Question

I miss the way you looked at me
like I might be the answer
to a question you forgot you'd been asking.

Apologies

I crept down to the riverbed to cry
about all the ways I cannot love you
and to say I'm sorry to the trees
for all the ways that I am not free.

Yours Someday

I feel you like a bass drum,
a thrumming in my soul,
a hum from miles away.
Even now, as the ringing in my ears fades to black,
I can hear your name in mountain bells.
And I still believe I will be yours, someday.

Divine Static

The words are there today
on the other side
of the thinnest veil.
I need only to find the solvent
to dissolve the breath between myself
and the All of creative flow.

I need only allow the pen to lead,
and heart to beat how it wants
to see the vision
and not *need* to see it.

Write without the urgency
but with steadfast commitment.
No expectations, all availability.

I have no claim to these pieces,
their beauty or horror
is only divine static
caught on paper.

Like Falling

I became a poet
like I became your lover,
without thought
without intent.
Just a simple giving way
to the inevitable.

Don't Shine

I keep the shine to a minimum most of the time.
The supernova in my chest is blinding and hot
and I want you to feel me as a soft, cool stream.

I am body parts barely held together,
all string and willpower.
I fly apart without thinking,
shards of earth-being scattered
to the ends of my imagination.

I can see the Milky Way
far behind my left ear
and my toes dangle beyond
the nebula where I lived 10 lives.

Yes, I keep the shining to myself when I can,
'cuz it's hard to love a galaxy blown apart,
and hard to trust a million pieces of chaos.

It's far easier to taste my warm skin,
tracing letters on my back
and lifting the hair gently from my neck
to kiss the secret nape.

I want you to hold me.
Hold me so I don't fall apart.

Monsters

Ya know,
sometimes I think we're all
just insecure monsters,
hoping someone will find
our monstrous side lovable, too.

Hollow Bones

Imagine how it feels to have bird's wings.
To pick up your empty bones
and let the wind carry you
to the waiting flock.

Bitterness

When heartbreak is all you can taste,
go into the semi-sweet longing
and let it flood your mouth
with chocolate kisses
and old coffee grounds.
You will know when
it is time to move on.

When you are ready
for a new palette,
drink cold water,
squeeze lemon on the sugar cubes
and let the fresh burst of sweetness
linger on your tongue
reminding you of renewal,
and of spaciousness.

Please remember
that none of us are meant
for bitterness all the time.

Joy

Joy decided to join me today.
She had been hiding among the roots
in the vegetable garden.
She had been dancing
with frogs in the pond.
She had been ice skating
around the frozen tundra
on the other side of the world.

And I had almost forgotten her warm harmonies.
The way she makes everything lighter.
I could hear her whistling through
the deepening green of summer branches,
and I felt soft breezes
caress my tender heart.
My brow softened
and my jaw unclenched
and I welcomed her home
with a sigh.

Soft Animals

I am the softest animal,
jellyfish bones and rabbit eyes.
Belly open, heart bleeding into the earth.
I have learned to find shelter behind rocks and under
shells,
to raise my arms flinching for the blow.
Prickly spines have grown in places
that need defense most often,
calloused fingers guard the edges
from near constant barrages.

I am the softest animal,
and my journey is always back to softness.
To remove the quills, put down the shields,
to stand in the open spaces this way.
So that I may do no harm in my attempt to survive.
So that I may encourage gentleness in those around me.
There is courage in disarming oneself
and choosing love amidst the sharpest moments.

Miracles

I'm holding miracles between my teeth,
checking each one for gristle
before I swallow them whole.

Imperfect

I'm scared of losing you.
The way I am scared
of forgetting myself
or the way you wake in the morning
and suddenly realize that most of your life
is behind you.

I want you to love me,
the actual me.
The me that gets angry sometimes
when you're not taking
your own safety seriously
or when your positive thinking
is ignoring systemic injustice.

I want you to love me as a mother.
As a partner.
As a woman who is strong
and smart beyond expectations.
I want you to love my sharp truth
and the teeth I try my best to hide.

I am scared of losing you because
you've decided to adore a version of me,
while I love the entire whole of you.
I deserve more than adoration
or admiration for assimilation,
for being the perfect girl.

I am an imperfect woman
And I can only be with people
who see how much better that is.

Ellipses

You left me with an ellipses,
a cliffhanger,
a maybe someday…
I'd say it's the not knowing
that's been the hardest,
all the stories I created
about why you disappeared.

But the hardest part is how
I just plain miss you.
Simple and pure as a baby
reaching for a mother's face.

Missing you is the sweetest water,
the greenest field,
the most beautiful bird call.
It is nature at its most untainted.
Love cannot be snuffed by removing
the oxygen from the room -
It is self-sustaining.

And sometimes on morning walks
I still talk to you.
And sometimes you post poems
with the same words as mine
in a different configuration...
And I know that we are still connected.

And I rest in the assurance
that there is nothing you can do
about that.

Polar Flip

When I talk to god about you,
god tells me stories of the beginning of times
and how we were both there
and how we will still be here at the end.

The end is in fact where we met,
to bring about the beginning again.
We are the turn, the polar flip
so it makes sense that it feels a bit like we
pull the world together and apart all at once.

Poetry Whispers

Awaken the words with silence,
with ease and empty days and bare feet.
With slow strolls and early mornings
and cups of tea.

Poetry likes to whisper,
You have to listen or you'll miss it.

Spring

I think the season
has finally turned.
Grey notes are fading
and spring is
humming itself to life
after winter spats
and icy turns of phrase
we should've left
in the mall parking lot.

Our small creeks run faster
toward summer kisses,
and these legs wrapped tightly
'round your hips.
The southern winds
are blowing me to you,
and your scent, like honeysuckle,
smells like home.

Boundaries

Boundaries mean saying "no"
to things you want to do, too.
Not every opportunity is yours
within this moment.
Release and then release some more
until your plate has space for you.

Behind the Waterfall

I find myself behind the waterfall,
with all the chaos and noise
of this busy world
blocked out by
cascading waters.

I am alone here
in dark, wet caverns
with a small lantern
and just enough light
to see my own breath.

My thoughts echo in the sacred emptiness
and I can feel my own heartbeat reverberating
down tunnels and into lost sanctuaries
and healing pools buried deep in the earth.

I rest in the sanctity of this cool escape
and let my unseen self run free.

Expectations

I love you
but I don't want your life.
I am happy with my simple writing desk,
my overflowing love,
my small dreams.

7/10

I used to do handstands in the pool,
feel up straight and tall, with toes pointed.
My mother would rate me out of 10,
pretending it was the Olympics.
It was only years later that I realized
that she was rating me that way
out of the pool, too.

Mother

I stood in the kitchen,
black and white tile, bare feet.
Terra cotta walls and the tiles
you brought home from Spain.
Little windmills embedded into the walls.

All I felt was you.
You and your intense glare,
your warm laugh,
and your silver hair.

You weren't the kind of mother
to bake cookies
or come to sports games.
You were harsh and real,
determined to make me into a woman
who would survive in this world.

You kept your earrings
in a box that rotated,
with my baby teeth saved inside.

The front drawer of your dresser
had a little red lint brush in it.
I used to take it out and pet it
like a small, furry creature.
Somehow it made you feel softer.

Crawling under the covers
when there was a storm,
the only time you'd let me get in bed with you.
No wonder I still love the rain.

The Father

Remove the stain of your indifference.
Wipe clean the pain of your distraction.
Your selfish way of driving past
the last exit on the freeway
despite my full bladder.
You actually have the nerve to smile
as you take away
the last shred of control I had.

I am angry and bloody and worn,
a warrior child with knives for fingernails.
I am clawing down the door
to my own wholeness,
and escaping rooms of neglect
after years of waving to you
through mirrors and windows.

Your shadow is all I've ever known.
The solid, steadfast masculine eluded me.

I have become my own father now.
Replenished, safe,
defending my own bright light from onlookers,
closing curtains to shield my naked silhouette.

Innocence reclaimed.
I nod to you from afar and decide
you deserve no more than my cool goodbyes.

Familiar Aches

I saw the best in you
and you saw the worst in me.
What an ordeal.
I often wonder why I chose it,
and of course I did.
We always choose the ache
that feels most familiar.

This Same Game

I pull you around to face me
nose to nose, soul to soul
and I tell you I struggle with trust,
with abandonment,
with a fear that love
is not only not just enough,
but also part of the problem.

You tell me you love me.
That I can trust you.
That you won't leave.

And then you leave.

And who can I even blame
but myself
for choosing this same game,
on repeat
under the guise
of healing?

How Are You, My Love?

I will wonder about you sometimes,
when I drink from mountain streams or
see the sunlight casting shadows
through the willow tree.
My heart will open
and I will ask a question
of cool solitude,
"how are you, my love?"

Rawr

Our love is petrified in amber
and buried deep within the layers
patiently awaiting us
to extract its DNA
and resurrect its enormity.

Identity Maintenance

I am done being different people
depending on the context.
I am hereby relinquishing
the idea of identity maintenance.
I want to know my entire soul,
and i have no idea how to do that
while simultaneously hiding
in plain sight.

Growing Pains

If I sit still long enough I realize
that my heart is always breaking.
It's an ache in the center of my being,
like a beacon.
Love and pain are the same feeling.
That deep stretching in my heart
like it's always trying to grow.

Fiction

I want the kind of freedom
you can only feel in fiction.

I want to write the kind of fiction
you can only feel from living freely.

Exhale

I will bend around your longest exhale,
placing dreams in each of your open palms
alongside your morning coffee.

The Open Window

I want a dog and a patch of sun,
long hair and lemonade.
I want a story that flows out of me
and resonates to the tune
of real currency in the world.

A published book,
money for travel,
time and space and quiet.
Laughter with good friends.
Deep kisses and a partner who
looks at me like I hung the moon
and then goes to wash the dishes.

I want a view that is nothing but trees
and a child who runs barefoot to the creek.
I want to live in Paris
and smoke a secret cigarette once every 5 years
in the arms of a lover I met on the train.
I want dark chocolate
and the knowledge that I
made a real difference in the world.

What about you?
If you let go of everything you're supposed to be,
who is left standing by the open window?

The Key

I thought I was the key
but I was the ocean
waiting for the door to be unlocked.

Beautiful Beast

I am desperate to feel something
besides this gnawing loss,
besides this tasteless melange
of daily life without you.

It's like food without salt.

And I know I will get over it.
The heart is a strong and beautiful beast.
She will always find new steak
to tear at with tiny, loving jaws.

Can I Be New?

Can I be the sapling, tender and lean,
vulnerable and trusting of the wind,
the grasshopper, the beetle?

Can I lift my chin and let the tears
dry on my face as I watch
the moon ebb and flow
in night skies?

Can I let my life be slow,
boring, simple?
Can I release my hold on complexity
as a form of justification?

Maybe.
Maybe I can rest here,
like a child of the universe,
in awe of my own existence.

Flavor of Joy

Let yourself ripen on the vine.
Sunlight, water, stillness, safety.
Growth comes when we are fed.
Change comes when we stop trying
so hard to become.

Turn your face to the sun and drink it in.
Soak up the rain.
Don't hurry maturation-
you are the perfect flavor of joy
right this moment.

The Paradox of Surrender

I love to talk about love
how it asks as much as it gives,
how it only sticks if you release it,
how it only lands if you allow yourself to fall...

Spidery Things

Sometimes I wish my poems were happier.
Meditations on how to live life well or
notes on finding the beauty in things.

But my poems are usually little spidery things,
that crawl out of the darker spaces of my mind.
I love them in their dusky awkwardness,
all legs and shadows limping toward the sunlight.

In Love with Writers

For years I was always falling in love with writers,
the romance of it;
to be in someone's thoughts,
to see yourself in their words.

And now I have become the thing I love.
I've taken the adoration and scooped it into my lap.

The ultimate act of self-love has been owning my passion
without outsourcing it to another.

Becoming a writer is the deepest claiming
of myself that I can imagine,
the truest form of honesty
I can conceive of in this lifetime.

Earthkin

She was Earthkin, a forest walker -
tuned into the fox den and the sparrow nest.
She talked to the Maple tree on the corner
by the bookstore,
whispered secrets into the stony bark.
And it spoke to her in hushed leaves
of the coming Autumn,
of letting go,
of small deaths.
She felt herself shedding layers,
preparing for her own kind of fall.

Love Junkie

There is nothing I love more than love.
I am a total love junkie.
Tell me about every person you love
and I will love them along with you.

The Color of Everyday Things.

I see the world from far away most of the time,
like a map below me with little heat signatures
telling me exactly where emotions are running hot.

But there is another view I can take.
A view made up of the tiniest details:
The sound of bubbles popping against the can,
or the way the breeze comes in from the window
and strokes my right cheek.

The way I can't look at the camera when I think,
having to turn my head
to go inward,
as I dislike being watched.

I see the world with my eyes, my hands,
and that satisfying click of the shutter.
There is a light that shines around the
edges of your face
making it separate from the background.

The color of everyday things,
the tiny, shining moments
that make up the terrain of this existence.

Map view or close-up,
it's an astonishing gift.

Night Watch

I am a wolven creature,
a solitary pack animal.
The one who wanders away
to howl at the moon
but secretly wants you to join her
with moonlight kisses
and cups of peppermint tea.
I want to nuzzle in
and finally release the need
to keep the night watch alone.

Sober

I've woven back the clock
by removing alcohol from the menu.
I see myself in slow motion then,
the whiskey taking my needs down a notch
until my speech is slurred
and I forget how desperate I am
to become someone.

I am stretching out the days now
and tending to the honesty,
the aching reality of never being numb.

It takes practice to live this way,
fully awake to the pain.
But here is the fresh, red truth:
I love every minute of this raw, real world

My Own Garden

I want to rest gently
in my own garden,
with my wild animals
and my wild thoughts.

One More Week

All I want is one more week with you.
To make sure we aren't right together.
To make sure your breath
isn't the lifeforce I believed it to be.
One more night of looking at the stars
upside down with nowhere else to be.

One more moment
when your eyes followed mine
around the room
trying to imagine
how to see the world
as one body in two forms.

All I want is to know,
to really know
that we aren't meant
to know each other.

But what I have instead
are these words,
made holy
with their inexhaustible longing.

Free

Thinking back on it now
I'm not sure I was in love with him
as much as I was in love
with a freer version of myself.

(and I got to keep her)

Not Wasted

Everyone I love
becomes a part of me.
Sometimes I think
that's exactly
what love is.

-No love is ever wasted.

Dance

Dance until the agony that has attached
itself to your bones shakes free.
Dance until the trees sing your name
and the sky spins
with the color of your eyes.
Until the ground pulls you
to your knees
in surrender and laughter.

Let the leaves bury you,
and dark berries soak
into your white clothes,
your hair, and your hands.
Rest in the cool, sacred earth
until you forget you were ever torn asunder.
Roots sew your heart back together,
good as new.

.

Cold Feet

I ache for moonbeams
and indigo-flavored glaciers.
I am drawn to the darkness
like stars with cold little feet.

Phantom Guitar

The strings on my guitar buzz almost inaudibly
when trucks roll by outside my window.
Little quakes in the foundation,
a humming in my belly.

I miss the flow of magic that opened
like a bridge of light whenever I heard your voice,
the jolt of pure, unadulterated joy
I felt at seeing your face.

You are a buzzing in my soul.
Cosmic guitar strings still humming
with phantom memories of your soft strum.

Kissing Strangers

I miss kissing strangers
and rooms full of bodies
moving to a beat
you can feel in your belly.

There is a heat to humanity
that means we are alive.
A kinetic energy like lightning
that holds the key to our
wellbeing.

Press into me and remind me
that we will one day dissolve into
wholeness once more.
Molecules dancing together
in the ether.

Oblivion

When we come together again
I will kiss you 'til the stars collapse
'til the world tilts toward oblivion.

Electric Breaths

The flash comes 7 seconds before the rumble.
I wait for it, letting the silence between lightning
and thunder make up the cells in my body
like the moment between a question
and an answer.
Like the moment between knowing
you're having an orgasm
and the actual release.
The space that is and isn't
like life itself - here and gone at once,
just electric breaths
between light and sound.

Little Mammals

Wake the animal within
from its cozy slumber
and ramble through the redwoods,
down the path, to the edge of the cliff
where your mother once stroked
your unbrushed hair and pointed out
the constellations she could remember.

Little mammals holding hands
and counting just how small we really are.

Surround Me

Surround me with pine needles
and make a bed of acorns and thorns.
When things are too comfortable
I cannot feel the will of the words,
and poetry reigns queen in these woods.

Easy Love

I love more easily and deeply than most.
I fall in love with sun-drenched mornings
and apricots,
with the way your eyes shine
when I tell you my secrets.
I fall in love every day,
all day long
and sometimes it aches in a way
I don't think I can stand,
but I wake up every day and do it again.

Unburdened

I did a magic spell
to remove the stinger
from my skin.
A little chant
to douse the flames
of a passion
that had nowhere to go.

I took my grief on a 14-hour road trip
and buried it in the backyard of my parents house
under tall weeds and deer netting.

I kept the love
but left the slowly
burrowing ache
in the soil
to return to where it
came from.
I released you
and drove back home.
Unburdened,
new,
healed.

Ribcage

I have opened,
less like a door
and more like a ribcage.
A cracking and breaking
to rediscover a flow.
I am bruised and aching,
but stronger and more alive.

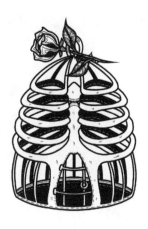

Shatter

God, I want to be seen. Touched. Known. Loved.
I want to be scooped out like ice cream.
Taste my sweet milk and swallow me whole.
Tear me apart with your fingers
and lick the sticky juices
of my undoing.

I want to be challenged, tested,
confused, unloosed.
I want you to rebuild me
over and over again, like legos.
Like a stencil, like art.

I am a million pieces of colored glass,
rearrangeable and complex.
A puzzle with infinite solutions,
each one an image of divinity.

I get lost in a perfection
that can only exist as fantasy.
Let me be the one to love you whole.
I am mere reflections
of the very best parts of yourself.

Liquify and recoagulate,
blood and bone
and heartbreak upon heartbreak.

I shatter to realign.

Cellophane Year

I got so sad last night remembering
all that we are missing.
The sharing of tables,
that clink of silverware
and handing off wooden bowls of salad.
Even the awkward moment
when someone arrives late
and we all stand up to say hi at once.

I am so sick of being wary,
watching my distance,
where I put my hands, and my mouth.
I crave recklessness and candor,
the swimming in other's breath,
the lack of fear,
and the honest, unbridled joy
of human contact.

This year feels wrapped in cellophane.
A plastic bag you can't get open
without using your teeth.
I want to break through,
skin to skin
heart to heart
face to face.

Wildfire

I am wildfire and honeycomb,
burning trees and dripping sweetness.
I am street lamps and deserted highways.
I am basement beer pong.
I am faultless irony and glimmering wit.
I am the girl in the flowing dresses.
and the one who walks home with a secret smile.

Blush of Poetry

Heart flutters, winged mayhem.
All fear and fluster and lightspeed.
All dust and clutter and birdseed.
I want to drape myself over the fountain
and feel the water drip into my mouth,
fresh and clean, a lifting away of all these ashes
that cling to my hair.
Hair in mouth like spiders
crawling in the bedsheets.
I fall back into the grass
and watch the robins hopping
in the sunbeams.
Earth and mud and the bluest of clouds.
I feel a dark shift rising in my chest,
a freedom that comes with saying "fuck it" to safety,
to words that make sense.
A blush of poetry, like nightfall,
like moonshade, like bird song.

Colored Dresses

I hang my brightly colored dresses up
where I can see them.
Little reminders of being seen.

I live in red and blue and yellow.
Bright jewel tones
of glass beads and candy jars.
But I think in grey and brown
and cream and eggshell.
Delicate, in-between shades,
layers of linen and muslin.

I sense the smallest changes
in your tone or timing
and I know when something is in the air.

I smell emotions like petrichor,
earth turned coffee grounds,
dark roast with rain and unresolved tension.
I know when your soul changes colors, even a little.

Love lives in these small shifts,
like the fluttering of light through
sheer curtains caught in summer breezes.

Breadcrumbs

I walked through the woods,
your scent following me
through the Elder trees.
I can't seem to shake you.
Haunted.
No matter how hard I try
to cover my tracks
I keep leaving pieces of myself behind,
breadcrumbs for the hunter.

Being Loved

For some of us, being loved
and feeling loved
are two very different things.

North Winds

Clawing at the door,
I hunger for intimacy,
raw and wild with no sense of shame.
Owning it all.

I want to tear you apart
with teeth glistening
and smiles as wild as the North Winds.

I am not what I seem,
I am the she-wolf.
I need touch to open
to the agony,
chest flayed,
and lives spent waiting
for the key to my domestication.

A Wilder Horse

I can taste your sadness from here.
An attempt to cover pieces long revealed,
to back out of being lead in the school play.

I miss you.
The glee in your voice,
trepidation now...
and I can't blame you.
I can only hurt you.

That is my continued fate -
innocence cannot survive here,
nor purity, or a simple version of the truth.
I am the wild unknown, untamed and savage.
I belong to no one.

Run with me like
wild horses galloping toward red rocks
and black sand beaches
but don't try to saddle me or
I will leave you broken in the dust,
tears streaming down my face
as I disappear into the horizon.

Dear One,

I see you there with your fingers
clutching at life like a security blanket.
Soften, soften now to the possibility
that you must let something go.

Holding tightly will do nothing
but cut off the streams of love
that flow so tenderly, freely,
voluntarily around your rocky outcroppings.

You must surrender to the possibility of loss
so that the reality of love can exist without restraints.
Release your grip and your belief
that you can control anything.
Relax, unclench your fist, let go.
Breathe. Love. Repeat.

Proof of Tides

I am like the salt that
dries from the sea.
The evidence left behind
of enormous movement.
The proof of tides.

Fire Ants

His apathetic silence
covered fire ants in his chest.
A rising sea of broken glass
and bloody footprints in the sand.

He couldn't speak
for the snakes coiled
tightly around his ribs.

Her eyes, grey now
with disappointment and confusion,
moved sadly away,
never knowing what he wanted to say.

Depths

There are no depths
I'm afraid of entering anymore,
no spaces that feel more dangerous
than my own self-forgetting.

Venus Flytrap Eyes

Gazing into the horizon
waiting for you to come
gliding into my view.

A snapshot with each blink,
I can see us move in double time,
an old movie reel
of laughter and heartache.

It is more poison than honey
for us both in the end.
I open my lashes
and watch you fly away.

Sometimes going hungry
is the safer bet.

Orange Groves

I keep trying to release you
leaking you out of my eyes and
washing you out of my tangled hair.
I am so ready to let go,
but you live in my very cells
and I have no idea how to set myself free
from someone who made my entire being
feel like sunshine and orange groves.

Beyond Measure

I keep falling in love with vast spaces:
the sky, the stars, the ocean, you.

I sometimes feel small
when they keep doing what they do
without taking much notice of me…

And then, I breathe the warm wind into my lungs
and sigh with relief
as the infinite within
my own beating center
reminds me that my love,
too, is beyond measure.

The Aspen Grove

Leaving behind the silken robe
in the aspen grove,
I wander naked into the starry night
and find again that when I am alone
I am never lonely.

It is only when I reach for you
and feel the empty bed
that I cannot seem to sink back
into my own breath.
A craving for touch,
and longing for forgiveness.

But here, in the field,
among the windswept romance
of haunted houses,
I am at peace.
And I am still and calm
within the tornado,
so sure that it will quell
my gnawing need
and sooth my simple ask:
to love me as I am.

Miss You Forever

I want to miss you forever
and I know I will forget.
And it's the forgetting that scares me most.
The magic of you, of us,
will fade to a distant point on the horizon
I can barely recall.
The notes of our melody will become
lost to my muscle memory.
I don't want to put our love in the closet
with my other lost passions to collect dust.
I would rather ache and cry
and grasp at the sliver of hope,
slender and curved as the nearly new moon,
that maybe, just maybe you are still part of my future.

The Garden

I am unwinding the knots
from my childhood,
the ones that still reach
to the back of my neck,
tender and twisted like roots
from the original tree.

I am tending to the gnarled parts.
The bits that have molded to my spine.
I wonder if it is time for the pruning shears,
a quick snip to the nape of the mangled mass
of broken ties and curving
highways of desolation and neglect.

So that I might stand of my own accord.
So that I might lift my chin and see
that other connections are waiting for me
to release myself from ancient groves.
From old stories and myths of feelings
that take over buildings
and tear them to the ground
with a need for attention,
for water, and for love.
I am ready to leave the garden
for the wild and unkempt paths
of the woods beyond the past.

Sugar Beets

A loving energy coaxes me out of hiding
with sugar beets and colored glass,
with ocean songs and creaky screen doors.
I feel the love encircling me
and whispering new musings
gently in my ear:
You are beloved, whole, holy,
and wild as nightscapes.
You are teardrop.
You are dove coos.
You are morning coffee and mountain air.
You are imperfect and deeply flawed.
You are loved and held in every moment,
Never alone, never shameful.

Quit You

You reminded me more of bourbon
than I thought was possible.
Warm and sharp,
taking my pain away,
and flooding my system
with comfort and pleasure.
I felt more myself than ever.

And then the crash would come
and I was left thirsty and alone,
Stomach-churning anxiety
and dread that made me realize
I'd have to quit you, too.

Wholeness Party

When you feel depleted, close your eyes
and reach for the tender parts of yourself
that linger with those you've loved,
and gently (so gently) invite them home.

Their return will feel like sunshine.
Embrace each piece
and give them honey cakes and lemonade.
Throw a party for your wholeness.

Potion for Moving On:

I already have a bathtub full of tears
And fistfuls of of sage from a priestess
I knew in San Diego.
I have already howled at the moon
and danced naked around the fire.

I have penned a million words about
our love and loss.
I am just waiting for the alchemy, the
transformation, the magic puff of smoke
that makes this ache mean something.

I suspect I am missing the final ingredient:
a single word from you.

Grief

I urge the words to swell into waves of language
that take this pain and turn it into poetry.
Create something beautiful
before it fades completely
into ash and cardboard
inside my mouth.

I miss the bright pain, fresh and red like blood on lips.
I miss the slicing ache, the sharpest pangs,
the relentless belief that I will hear your voice again.

This duller ache, born of time and hopelessness,
feels like a betrayal,
an erasure of the magnitude of our love.
I prefer the crisp, clean whip of heartbreak to the
slow, numb emptiness of learning to live without you.

Not Ok

I go looking for inspiration now
that I've lost your voice.
I stare at the ceiling,
my kitchen table,
all the places where air comes in
through the cracks under doorways.

It used to be so easy to find a place to start:
your eyes, your smile,
the way the world made way for us to meet, to fall in love.
Every piece of it felt intentional, placed for my noticing.

And now I search, half-blind from grief,
for pieces of beauty I might find
buried in the pine needles.
I go searching for my joy and find my pain
lounging in the sunlight where our future used to be.

And I knock on doors,
borrowing cups of tea from the neighbors
hoping someone will ask me how I'm doing,
so I can finally say, "I'm not ok."

Over You

So, I'm not over you yet.
Your voice is like sunshine to me,
reverberations, enlightenment,
scattered rainbows that illuminate
pieces of me I'd forgotten in dark corners:
innocence, simplicity, child-like joy.

I gather them to me,
wrap my arms around them
and try to remember that I am
allowed to feed them even when
you are not here to witness it.

Lips

My unconscious mind drifts to your lips,
it's annoying.
I have other things to do,
but that's all there is to it some days.
A series of distractions from my life purpose.

This body, it takes so much tending;
feeding, touch, love, air, intrigue, magic, conversation,
reassurance.
And my mind can barely keep up with all the extras;
clean teeth, combed hair, small waistline,
and a series of clothes that go together.

It's exhausting this whole embodiment thing.
My unconscious mind reminds me now
that I chose this.
I chose to be here this time around,
and oh, not to forget
about the glory of your lips.

The Locket

She found the locket buried in a foot
of deep, dark viscera
and cleaned the gunk off with her thumb.

Inside was a face she recognized from another life,
eyes piercing and hair in long braids.
It closed with a crisp snap and she tucked it away
in her apron pocket, wiping the blood on her inner thigh.

She cut her teeth on yet another mystery,
burying pain and memories from other timelines
in the bread she pulled fresh from the oven.

She whistled for her soul and told it to lie down
by the kitchen gate and simply wait.
To wait for a love that may never come.

Becoming the Koi

I need you to understand that pain
is simply how I move through the world.
I am elbows and hip bruises.
I can't quite get a grasp
on the size of my edges.

Perhaps it is because
I don't think of my body
moving through space like others seem to.
For I am a giant heart with brains for ears,
just eyes and hands with nothing in between.
I collide with you, with anyone,
with whole rooms full of people
and then have to sort out
my own flesh from theirs.

It's exhausting.

I once watched a group of koi swimming in a pond.
They rushed to the edge, so used to being fed,
and I had to look away because I could feel their soft scales
crushing me,
and bodies sliding over mine.

Returning to softness yet remaining whole -
that is the trick I have yet to learn.

Stay Free

When you find your voice
you will also find that you receive a million invitations
to give away your power.

You will find yourself in situations, over and over again
where people encourage you to remain small.
These, too, are temptations.

It is much easier to lean back
and allow someone else to dictate your existence.
So much easier to fit in than to stand out.

When you find yourself at the precipice of freedom,
a cage will sometimes feel like a relief.

Don't fall for it.

Sometimes, when you have a traumatic past,
freedom will feel like abandonment.
It is not.

I Drop Down

I drop down,
head to heart
heart to gut.
On my knees.
On my back.
Floating waves of cotton candy dreams
and hourglass candles.

I drop down,
let it go:
my pride,
my walls,
the feeling of superiority,
any idea that I know more than my 5 year-old son
about the reason people hurt each other.

I drop down,
hands up,
feet splayed.
I cry for you to please
hand back the parts of me
you've been keeping in your locker
to show your friends after gym class.

I want to rise,
but first I fall.
I fall for you
and watch as I rebuild myself in your image,
a shiny moment of reconstruction
before the inevitable rejection
of a container meant for someone half my size.

I drop down into my own words
and burrow until I feel home
flowing through my veins.

Done Being Small

I am not a wife, I am a woman,
free like ice and large like sand castles.
I have vast worlds of need and anger
and power and life within me.
I am done being small for anyone.

Ruthless Truth

Here is the ruthless truth: I have no idea what I want.
I have no idea how to make this life taste like
cherry soda and poptarts.
I have no idea how to stretch my hand across
the spaces between
and finally touch something that feels like
true love, true living,
an honoring of this lifetime, this gift I've been given,
these words, these talents,
these trials, my own sense of safety, intuition.

Running across fields of lavender,
nose tickling from spring fever
And I am horse and trembling
trying so hard to find my place.

Spaces and lives blurring, I can't stay still -
there's another 3-legged race
at the other end of the faire.
Renaissance clothing and I am juggling now
the multitude of selves I could lean into
if I could only catch my balance.

If I could only sit in the warm grass and remember that
I am held in every moment.
That striving only wears me out and that my true calling...
that my true calling
is in my heart beating in tandem with yours.
Just that BaBoom BaBoom,
and the silence that follows.

John

I looked at you, you who has walked with me through almost 20 years of my life. You look the same, tall and handsome, so smart, so kind, with the softest eyes I've ever seen. I watch you with our son, a hundred times more patient that I could ever be. And I sigh with profound gratitude at this life, this love we have built.

It has not come carelessly, for we have been painstakingly gentle with one another. You, who couldn't plan a date if our lives depended on it, or do the taxes, or remember to call your mother. Me with my insane mood swings and inability to handle stress, light, sound, or a real job.

To say that we love each other isn't even fair to the word. It is so much bigger than love. It is a partnership of admiration, of freedom, of safety, and yes, sometimes of boredom, too. Each year we watch the other change, that is our only job really, to see it and say "yes, I still choose you" over and over again.

Heal

There are blisters on my heels
from walking so far in shoes
that don't quite fit anymore.
I take them off and leave
them by the side of the highway,
windows open, music loud,
and bare feet on the gas pedal.
And a lifetime to heal.

Home

I am home, in more ways than one.
Home from my trip, but also home in my bones.
Back from a larger trip through my own shadows,
excavating gemstones from dark spaces
and shining light into corners long abandoned

I find myself standing very still.
The air makes sound if you listen long enough.
Wind, like the subtle rush of blood in your ears.
The voice of life, of breath, of space, of love
whooshing by and through me.
Feet on earth, head in clouds,
I am home. I am truly home.

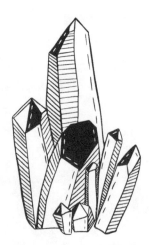

Scared and Sacred

Ringing mountain bells.
The sky opens in song and
I am queen of this small mound,
a fairy wish, a token at the end of the rainbow.
Pots of gold leaf and a mysterious smile
that guides you home.

Misty morning highways with epic redwoods
and twinkling lights high up in the trees.
Silver moon gladness and midnight kisses
with the man who holds your child's hand up
the side of steep cliffs.

Adventure is small things
and being willing to stay tuned in,
to listen to the all of someone.
To see past the hopes and fantasies
to the heart and soul of a human being;
scared and sacred at once.

Fresh Eyes

Tumbling through embodiment
with cuts and scraped knees
and hearts that bruise beyond repair
then find their way to health again, somehow.

You take my face in yours
and look at me like I am still new to you.
Nothing has ever felt more like love than being seen,
over and over again,
with fresh eyes, fresh love.

Narrow Place

I have been in a very narrow place,
a closed-in hallway, mostly dark, little air.
And I have recently walked into an open field,
no walls, no structure.
It's dizzying:
the freedom, the oxygen, the space.
I wobble and fall, no one to catch me. It hurts.

I am uncomfortable and free.
It takes me a few days to adjust to my new environment.
I find branches for fire and shelter,
berries to eat, soft grasses to sleep in.

But the stars, oh the stars!
I find my bearings there.
Like an ancient sea captain
I turn my wheel to the horizon
and follow my heart 'til morning.

A Subtle Light

Break harder, open deeper, ache longer.
Love with tears in your eyes
and blood on your hands.
Living lightly is false bullshit.
This here is a heavy timeline meant for heavy souls.
The denser the water,
the more at home I feel.
Sink into the depths toward the mud
and the salamanders,
and the filthy moss rocks and the black bark.
There you will find me shining.
I am a subtle light -
you need the darkness to see me.

Fallen Snow

I am a softly fallen snow,
white and quiet.
Your hands cup my face
and sculpt me into something resembling love.

I Become You

My skin doesn't hold my essence
It seeps out, permeable.
I leak into the waters, the earth
I evaporate, and condense again on your
morning cup of coffee.

I become you,
my cells adapting to the pace of your breath.
You want me to be myself,
but I am not an object to be known.
I am antimatter, ethereal and gaseous
Unpindownable,
(though I would enjoy being pinned down by you.)

I am pieces of everyone I've ever met,
mirror images, reflected love,
envy and raised eyebrows.
I see you as myself, my face as yours,
and for a time I become a solid.

I feel the ground,
your hands,
my heart is real and beating
and then you blink and I float away,
not empty
but weightless with the freedom
of enigmatic identity.

Burned

The ember leapt from the match
and fell into my lap,
singeing soft thigh skin.
I tried to brush it off
and it caught underneath my fingernail,
burning the untouched flesh
so carefully guarded there.

Ice water ran down my leg
to stop the burn,
but I could still feel you in my breath
like dragon flames.
Your love was like that tiny ember,
doing so much more damage
because it was so sudden and unexpected.

Artemis

I named my kitten, Artemis,
after the goddess of the hunt.
But she sits very still in the sun all day,
and rarely embodies anything close to wild.

It's me that is a wild thing,
a woman of the moon and arrow.
A warrior who demands freedom,
while seeking safety.

I don't like to be enclosed,
tied down - I need to submit freely, just ask.
Tip my chin to the moonlight,
eyes glowing feline,
ready to taste you.
To lick your wounds
and bury my face in your lap.

I am the wild one;
and my greatest cunning
is hunting only those
who come willingly.

The Seed

We are always the seed, the beginning,
the architect of creation, mothers of time.

I am fertile with no land to tend.
I want to throw my seeds into rich soil,
to water them with care,
But I get distracted by reality tv
and my desire to be adored, adorned even,
and made into an idol for you to worship.

I lose myself in the glory, in the ache to be seen.
I am a hunter, bow ready and feral to the bone.
I only have to strip naked and fearless,
removing mirrors completely,
going inward,
to find that apple seed,
and core from which it all grows.

I am fruited perfection,
ripe and sweet and ready eat;
ready to feed the world with a seasoned love.

Sensitive

I need to be alone.
Solitude. White room.
Emptiness.
My nerves unfurling, laying flat.
No needs. No expectations. No noise.
That is the only medicine for overwhelm sometimes.
The only way to find myself again when I feel lost

Expanded

I want to write the world into existence,
to tell wild stories that float to me in daydreams
while I'm doing the dishes.

I want to plant seeds in the ground and watch them grow,
chase bunnies out of gardens and tend the broken fence.
To lean casually against the barn
and watch the dogs chase each other in circles
around the wide yard.

I want to hear the sounds
of wooden spoons and casserole dishes,
To fall naked in your arms,
the rest of the world fading away.

I want to travel and cry and take in so much beauty
that my body explodes with the colors of rice fields
and marigolds and scarves in market places.

I want to feel the earth under my toes,
the rivers on my fingers, your breath in my hair
My shoulders bare and baking in summer suns.
Flowing skirts and unkempt hair
and twilight spinning behind my eyes.

I can't go back to pretending I am small.
I have expanded into the sea, floating wide and open
and gently, gently, I will flow around the rocks,
until they, too, become part of me.

Forgive Me

Bone tired, twisted romance
A million miles of empty highway
And my thighs ache from the gas pedal.

Cacti, tom waits and headlights
I delight in lyrics that sound like whiskey
and moonlight.

Soft white petals, mouth open and eager
On my knees now and wondering when
I lost my ability to set clear boundaries.

I feel tornado limbs and thistle brush hair
and I stumble home
to knock on the door of your room.
And pray you'll forgive me.

Cave Drawings

It's time to stop giving yourself away to the lowest bidder.
It's time to sit still, and to wait in dark waters
for your heartbeat to soften.
It's time to lift your face to the sunbeam
and stop worrying if anyone is watching or
what they think of your slow contemplation of the light.

Remember again, that the truth can only exist
between you and your higher self.
She who you met on a cold mountaintop in your mind
among pillars of stone and moss covered angst.
Crying out for someone to come
 and occupy your lonely bones.

It's time to pray only to her,
to the heart beating in your own chest.
Fingers interlaced in your own hair.
Take all that big love
and place it gently in the spaces inside,
so you'll remember who you are…
like cave drawings on the altar
of your own soul.

Secrets and Stars

She left the room quietly,
secrets and stars in her handbag,
absconding with the best parts of the buffet.

She sped away wearing velvet
from another woman's closet
She was called many names:
a thief of time,
a gambler of hearts,
and a liar through and through.

To say that she left them all broken
would be unfair.
She only took the pieces
that held them back
from being their best selves.

The loot was an afterthought.
It was the silence
that she took most delight in:
that moment when it all ended
and she could drive away
into the stillest of nights.

Printed in the USA
CPSIA information can be obtained
at www.ICGtesting.com
LVHW091813060924
790323LV00007B/742

9 780578 811109